CARTOONS BY
LAF

From the Original published in 1961

Eggbert is here again. Well, not quite here – but he'll be born soon. Meanwhile, he is developing and refining his definite and often unique ideas on love and life, digestion and indigestion, sex and even sisters. And Sis is wide-eyed with wonder at his wit and wisdom.
Whether you are expecting your own little one, or just expecting to laugh, Eggbert and Eggberta will not disappoint you.

Eggbert is a prenatal pixie. Whether you are expecting you own little pixie, or just expecting to laugh, Eggbert and Eggberta will not disappoint you.

Eggbert, and this small book, will take the Mother-to-be on a wondrous journey through morning sickness and doctors appointments to that amazing moment when she first feels life inside her; and sonograms and baby showers and preparing the nursery.

This book is a faithful reproduction of that original and it will keep the expectant Mom laughing all the way from the beginning of her pregnancy right to the big day when her little one enters the world.

We wish all Moms love, joy, fulfillment, and we provide this collection of cartoons as forever proof that humor is the best medicine in the world. Enjoy

EGGBERT AND EGGBERTA

A brand new edition
(Faithful to the original)

Printed with permission

Compiled by Judi Quelland

With gratitude to Susie Barker Lavenson,
Daughter of Percy Barker, the original publisher.

Original cartoons by LAF
Lester A. Friedman

Published 2016 using the material from the original Eggbert books.

Printed in the United States of America.

EGGBERT AND EGGBERTA

ADULT HUMOR FOR MOMS-TO-BE

HEY, MA ... HOW COME
I'M DOWN HERE, HUH ?

WELL, LET'S START WITH
THE BIRDS AND BEES...

HEY, MOM, TAKE A DRINK . . .
I'M THIRSTY!

I GO OUT THERE. SO WHERE IN
HELL DID I COME IN ?

COME ON, POP . . .
LAY OFF THE TICKLING !

BOY ! CAN WOMEN TALK DIRTY !

HEY, MOM, STRAIGHTEN UP !

BOY! SHE MUST BE TAKIN'
A NEW KIND OF VITAMIN !

MAN, WHAT I WOULDN'T GIVE
FOR A HOT DOG
WITH PLENTY OF MUSTARD !

IF I HANG ON 'TIL AFTER THE 25TH,
THEY WON'T BE ABLE TO RUN THAT
OLD GAG OF CHRISTMAS AND BIRTHDAY
PRESENTS COMBINED !

SHE'S PICKING A HELLUVA TIME
TO GO HOME TO MOTHER!

HOW'S ABOUT KICKING THE OLD MAN
OUT OF BED ?

FOR THE LOVA PETE, SWALLOW THAT DAMN PEANUT BRITTLE !

... AND JUST WHOSE FAULT IS IT
I'M DOWN HERE ?

YOU ARE TOO, FULLY EQUIPPED !

THAT DOC MUST THINK HE'S
TAPPING A WATERMELON!

NOTHING'S LOOSE. SHE'S SHOOTING CRAPS WITH THE MILKMAN!

OH BROTHER! SHE'S SWIMMING UNDERWATER AGAIN!

STOP SOBBING! ALL WE NEED NOW
IS TO GET HER HICCUPPING !

OKAY, KID ... READY FOR THE
COLD SHOWER !

BOY, WHAT A FUMBLE-BUM
THAT INTERN IS !

WHAT A CARD THAT DOC IS! MAKING
HER DIET TO KEEP ME SMALL !

STAY ON YOUR OWN SIDE !

"MEAT LOAF AGAIN," HE SAYS.
HE ORTA BE DOWN HERE!

HOW CAN YOU BE SEASICK ?
SHE'S ONLY TAKING A BATH !

OKAY, ONE MORE DANCE AND THEN
LET'S GET THE HELL HOME!

MAN ! IS SHE BITCHY TODAY !

YOU MIGHT AS WELL LEARN THIS NOW AS
LATER ... IT'S JUST AS EASY TO SNAG
A RUCH HUSBAND AS A POOR SCHNOOK !

IT'S GREAT THAT SHE'S PRACTICING WASHING THAT DOLL ... BUT THIS IS THE THIRD TIME SHE'S DROPPED IT!

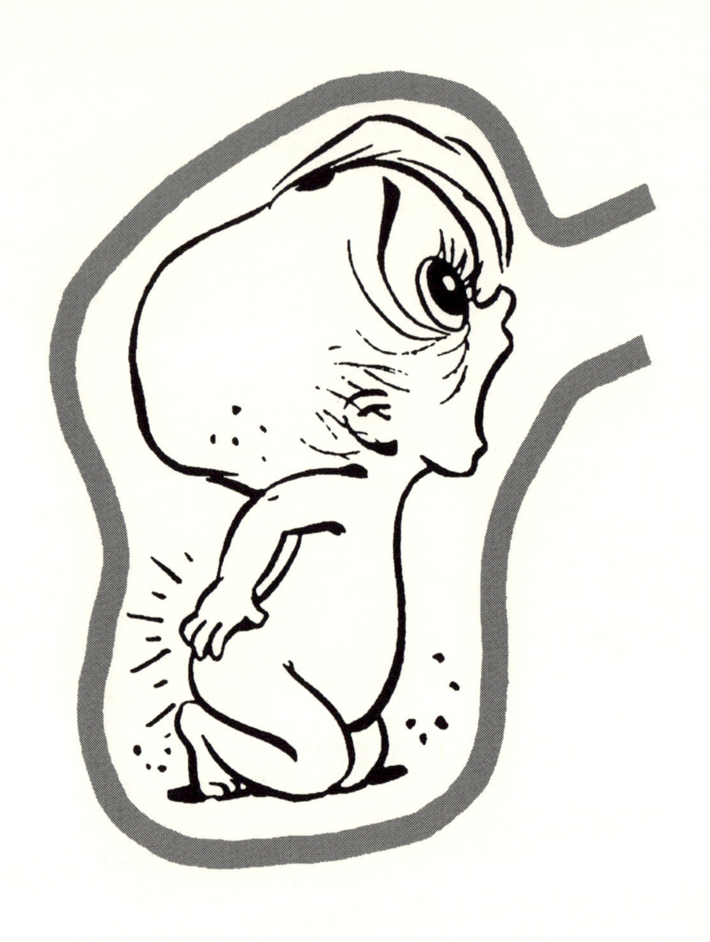

OUCH ! GET INTO THAT
HOT TUB A LITTLE SLOWER !

SURE IS COMFY WHEN SHE'S
GOT HER LEGS UP !

HOW CAN YOU CHEW A STEAK
WITH NO TEETH ?

MAYBE INSIDE ME IS ANOTHER LIKE ME
AND INSIDE ... AW, THE HELL WITH IT!

...I SAID, GET THAT GAW-DAMNED PURRIN' KITTY OFF YOUR LAP !

YOUR PULSE IS NORMAL ... AND I'LL BE DAMN GLAD WHEN MOM TAKES YOU OVER !

EWWWW! SHE'S
SUCKING LEMONS AGAIN!

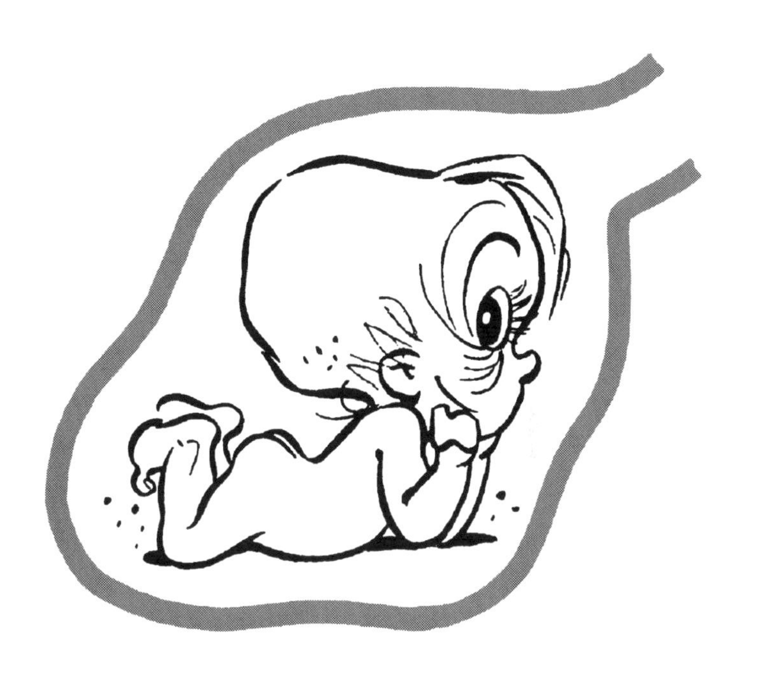

BOY ! THE RUCKUS I COULD RAISE
WITH A FEATHER !

I MAY BE A FULFILLMENT OF LIFE
TO MOM ... BUT JUST A LOUSY
1000-BUCK EXEMPTION TO THE OLD MAN !

STILL, I GUESS THIS IS BETTER
THAN WORKING FOR A LIVING !

WITH A LITTLE LIPSTICK AND
EYE-SHADOW ... YOU'D MAKE
A CUTE CHICK !

WHAT A WAY TO SPEND CHRISTMAS !

MICHELLE'S GOT A NEW HAIR-DO ...
THE MARKET OPENED STRONG ...
AND ALL HELL'S BUSTED LOOSE
AGAIN IN THE MIDDLE EAST !

AW, SHUT UP! MY FOOT'S ASLEEP!

OH, ME MOTHER WAS A LADY ...

WHAT THE HELL'S GOTTEN INTO YOU ?

MAN! SMELL THAT BACON!

I'M GONNA BE A STAR AND
I'M READY FOR MY CLOSE-UP !

C'MON, MOM ... BACK AWAY FROM
THAT BARBEQUE !

FIRST THING I DO WHEN I
GET OUT IS WRING THAT
EARLY-MORNING-CHIRPIN'
PARAKEET'S NECK !

COME TO THINK OF IT ... I'M A PRETTY
COMPLICATED LITTLE HUNK
OF MACHINERY !

COLIC ... MEASLES ...
MUMPS ... SWINE FLU ...
IF YOU ASK ME, I'M SAFER HERE !

HEY, MOM ... KNOCK ME OFF A LULLABY.
I CAN'T SLEEP!

YOU'D THINK THE LITTLE PUNK'D WAIT
UNTIL SHE'S BORN BEFORE
SHE STARTS TEETHING !

ONE SOLID HOUR ON THE CELL-PHONE
WITH THE DAMNDEST YAK I EVER HEARD !

I'VE BEEN IN HERE TOO LONG.
EVEN <u>YOU</u> LOOK GOOD TO ME.

... AND IF YOU THINK I'M RAISING
A RUCKUS DOWN HERE ...
WAIT 'TIL I GET OUTSIDE !

GO'WAN, LAUGH. BUT DON'T FORGET
YOU COULD BE IN MOM'S FIX
ANY MONTH NOW !

ZEESH! AND HE GETS PAID FOR THIS
KIND OF AN EXAMINATION, TOO !

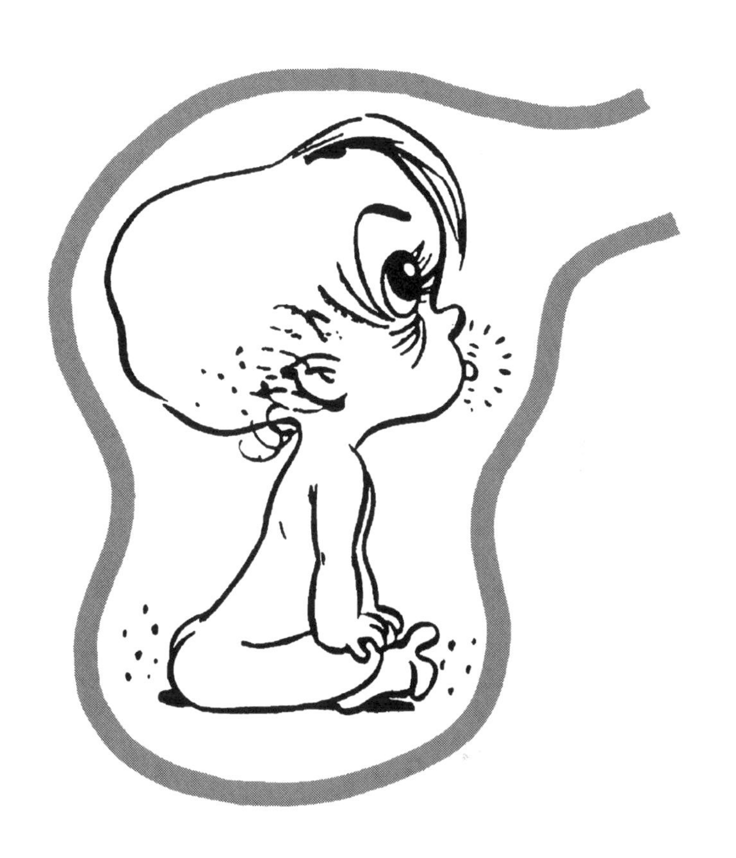

... AND TUNE THAT OUT
OF YOUR STETHOSCOPE !

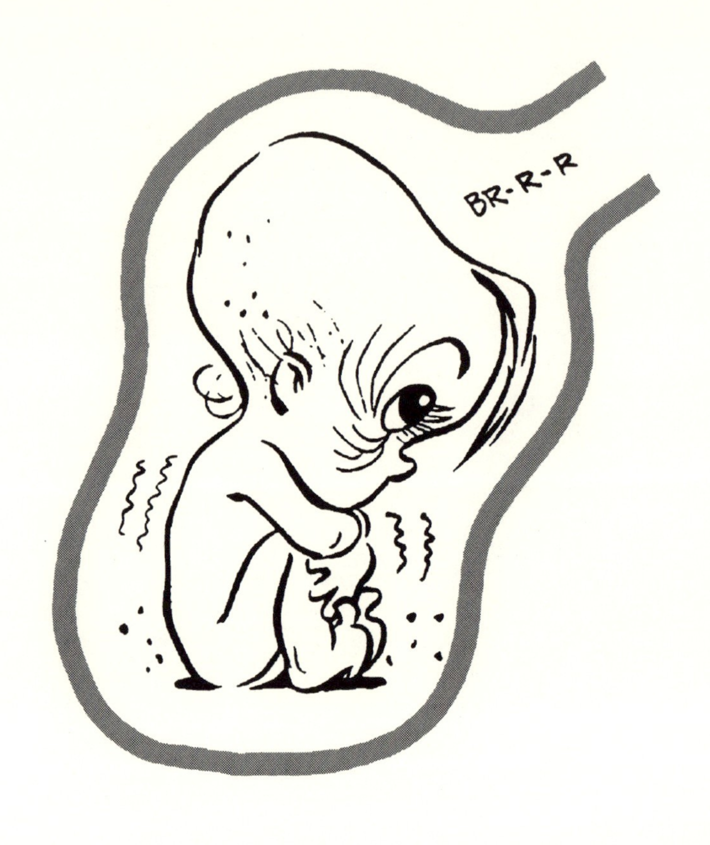

JUST ONCE ... JUST ONCE IS ALL I ASK
FOR A WARM EXAMINATION TABLE !

TODAY IT'S <u>YOUR</u> TURN TO LET DOC
LISTEN TO YOUR HEART !

IF YOU GOTTA SWIG ANOTHER
MARTINI, MOM, FOR THE LOVA PETE,
SIT DOWN !

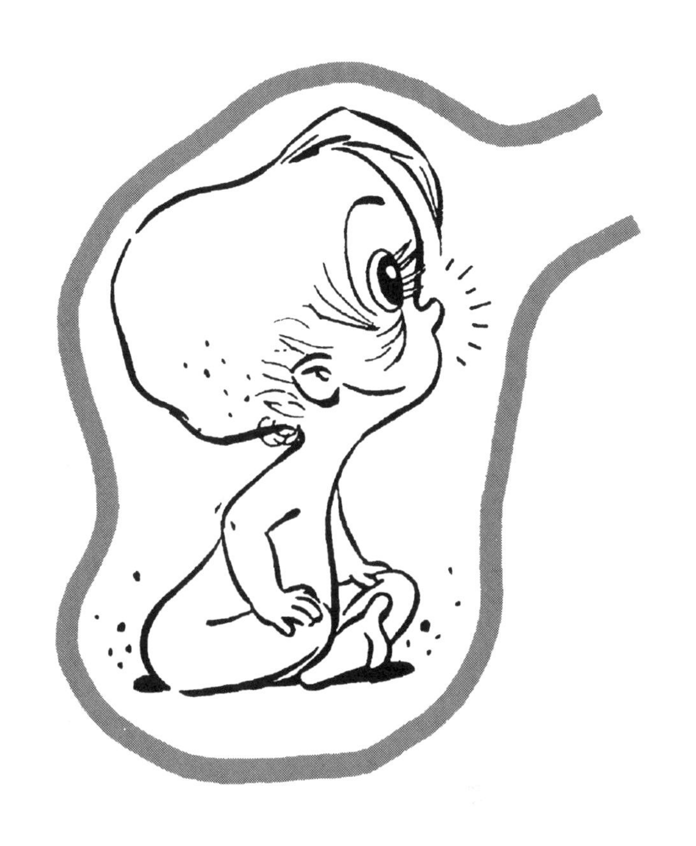

OH, MAN, ROAST CHICKEN! SHE'S AFTER
SOMETHIN' FROM THE OLD MAN!

. . . AND IF YOU DON'T LIKE MY CHOICE OF LANGUAGE - GET THE HELL OUT!

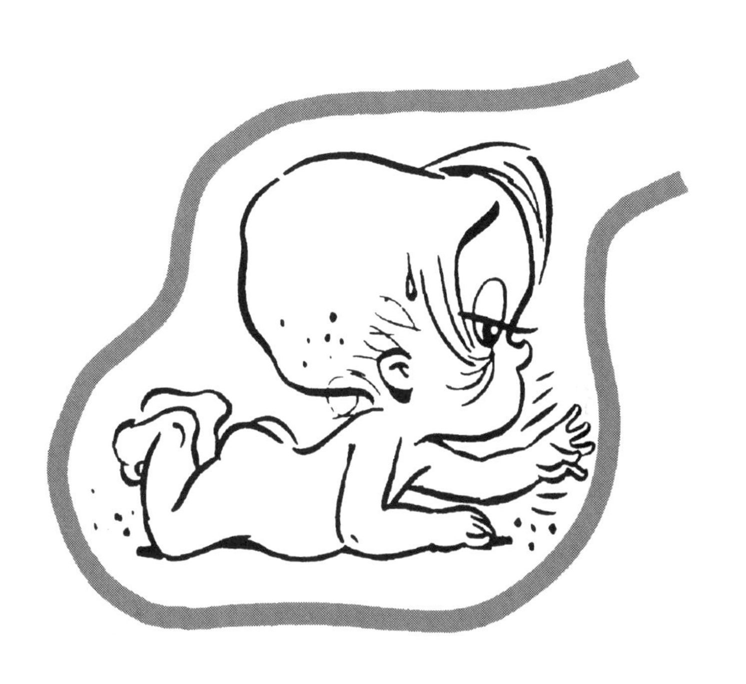

AW, C'MON POP, LAY OFF.
ME AND MOM HAD A HELLUVA DAY !

BOY ! SHE SURE HAD FOLLOW-THROUGH
ON THAT DRIVE !

WITH THOSE FANGS, YOU'RE A CINCH
TO BE A BOTTLE-BABY !

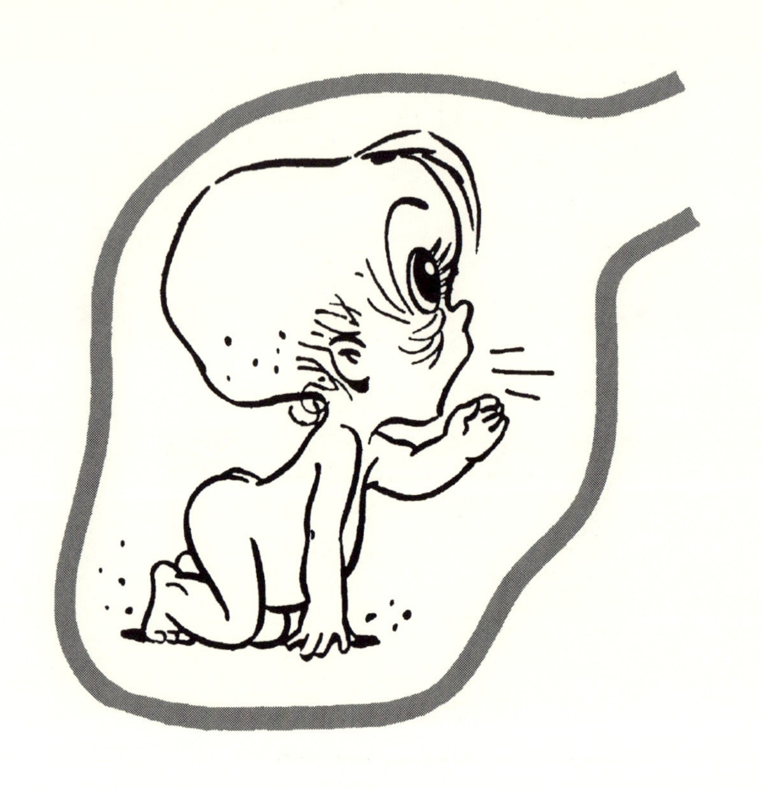

YOU TELL HIM, MOM ... THAT AIN'T
<u>OUR</u> SHADE OF LIPSTICK !

YEAH, AND YOU CAN TELL GRANDMA WHAT
TO DO WITH HER LITTLE PINK BOOTIES !

WHATCHA WANT AT YOUR AGE,
WATERMELONS, YET ?

MA AND I SURE MUSTA
HUNG ONE ON LAST NIGHT!

I REALLY GOTTA TAKE CARE OF MYSELF
TO KEEP THE FAMILY NAME GOIN' !

FOR A GIRL YOU SURE
GOT A BONY BACK !

WOW ! WHEN SHE'S NERVOUS, IT GETS NOISIER THAN HELL DOWN HERE !

I CAN SEE ME NOW. BEHIND THE WHEEL OF
A FERRARI ... THE TOP DOWN AND A
BLONDE CHICK IN THE OTHER BUCKET SEAT !

OH, COME OFF IT !

I GOTTA HAND IT TO THE OLD MAN.
EVERY TIME SHE LICKS HIM, BUT
HE'S BACK THERE SWINGIN'
THE NEXT EVENING !

... AND ANOTHER THING. NO EATIN'
ANIMAL CRACKERS IN THE CRIB, SEE ?

HEY, MOM ... CLOSE THE WINDOW OR
REV UP THE ELECTRIC BLANKET !

IF HE WASN'T OUR POP, DO YOU THINK
HE'D SHOW UP EVERY EVENING ?

BOY, ALL I'M GONNA DO THE FIRST
WEEK IS S-T-R-E-T-C-H !

LAY OFF ! WHO EVER HEARD OF
GETTING BORN IN AN M.G. ?

JUST AS I THOUGHT. MOM'S GOT INDIGESTION AGAIN!

SAY IT <u>AGAIN</u>, DOC ! ANY TIME
NOW ... WOWIE !

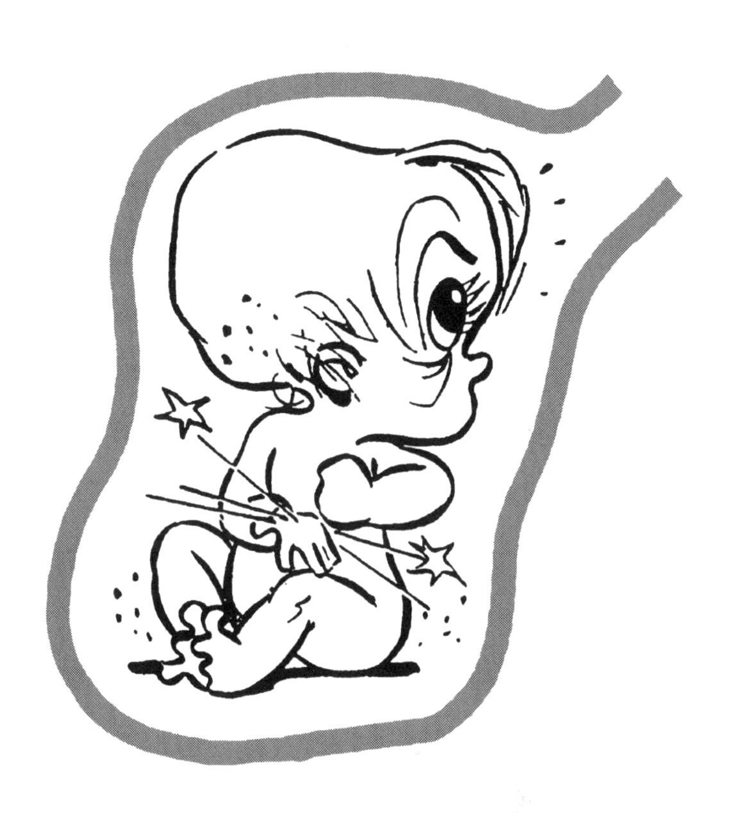

YOU'RE DARN TOOTIN' MOM
AND I WANT A PRIVATE ROOM !

I CAN'T WAIT TO SEE THE
OLD MAN'S EXPRESSION WHEN
I HAND <u>HIM</u> A CIGAR !

WONDER IF SHE SAVVIES
MORSE CODE ?

THEN I'LL SAY:
"YOU HAVEN'T FORGOTTEN
SOMETHING, HAVE YOU, DOC?"

AW, DRY UP ! YOU THINK SHE'S DOIN' THIS FOR A GAG ?

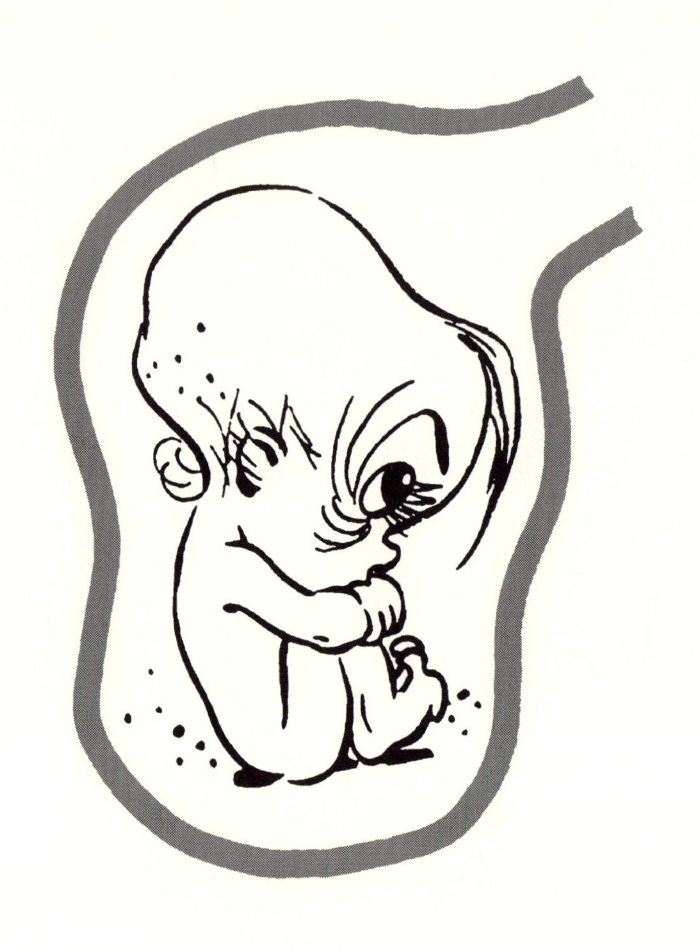

CRIPES ! SUPPOSE
THEY DON'T LIKE ME ?

IF THINGS LOOK OKAY, I'LL
WHISTLE YOU OUT!

HEY ! WHAT THE HELL'S
THE RUSH !

NOTES

NOTES

NOTES

Made in United States
Orlando, FL
24 January 2022